THE THOUGHTS OF MY LABRADOODLE

5 Year
Monthly Planner
2020-2024

DID I EVER TELL YOU

I love you hooman

Photo

DOGGY LANGUAGE

There's an entire language devoted to dogs; this language is known as Doggo Lingo. It's how your dog speaks and thinks. It's a fun, positive celebration of dogs.

Doggo	Doggos come in a variety of sizes ranked by the size of their bork (bark). They range from the tiny yapper to a diminutive pupper, an average-sized doggo, and the biggest woofers and boofers.
Longboi	A long-bodied dog such as a greyhound.
Floofer/Fluffer	A very fluffy dog such as a Samoyed or Pomeranian.
Thicc boi	A chubby dog – more to love.
Smol boi	A little yapper.
Woofer	A big dog.
Loaf	A dog, slightly overweight, which resembles a loaf of bread.
Pupper	A puppy.
Heckin' bamboozled	Sometimes you bamboozle the dog, sometimes the dog bamboozles you. Heck.
Do me a frighten	When a doggo is worried , scared or confused, potentially in the presence of borks or woofers.
Doin' me a	Having an action performed on oneself.
Bamboozle	A deceiving trick.
Awoo!	Howling.
Hooman	A human being.

DOGGY LANGUAGE

Blep/Blop	When your pupper is tired and his tongue hangs out just a little bit.
Mlem	Doing a lick. Not to be confused with a gentle blop.
Bork	Barking his little head off.
Boof	Not quite a bork, not quite a sneeze; it's the small huffy sound of a dog who's getting ready to bork..
Maximum borkdrive	This is otherwise known as the zoomies, when your doggo is going so fast they're just a blur.
Chimken	Chicken.
Fren	Friend
Henlo	Hello
Snoot	The nose always knows, and the snoot was made for booping.
Boop!	Touching your pet on the nose. Frequently accompanied by saying 'boop!'

Me and the hooman and the new fren went for a walk. And we saw other woofers and I jumped into a mud puddle. Awoo!

About My Dog

Dog's Name: Bella

Date of Birth: 12/2/18

Breed: labradoodie

Colour: Golden / apricot

Gender: Female

Adoption Date: 14 /04/18

Weight: 3.51 kg — when she had her first jab

Breeder: Jackie merrel

Microchip No: 981000103706 09

Registration No: N/A

Rabies: No

Neutered/Speyed: yes

2020

January

Su	Mo	Tu	We	Th	Fr	Sa
			1	2	3	4
5	6	7	8	9	10	11
12	13	14	15	16	17	18
19	20	21	22	23	24	25
26	27	28	29	30	31	

February

Su	Mo	Tu	We	Th	Fr	Sa
						1
2	3	4	5	6	7	8
9	10	11	12	13	14	15
16	17	18	19	20	21	22
23	24	25	26	27	28	29

March

Su	Mo	Tu	We	Th	Fr	Sa
1	2	3	4	5	6	7
8	9	10	11	12	13	14
15	16	17	18	19	20	21
22	23	24	25	26	27	28
29	30	31				

April

Su	Mo	Tu	We	Th	Fr	Sa
			1	2	3	4
5	6	7	8	9	10	11
12	13	14	15	16	17	18
19	20	21	22	23	24	25
26	27	28	29	30		

May

Su	Mo	Tu	We	Th	Fr	Sa
					1	2
3	4	5	6	7	8	9
10	11	12	13	14	15	16
17	18	19	20	21	22	23
24	25	26	27	28	29	30
31						

June

Su	Mo	Tu	We	Th	Fr	Sa
	1	2	3	4	5	6
7	8	9	10	11	12	13
14	15	16	17	18	19	20
21	22	23	24	25	26	27
28	29	30				

July

Su	Mo	Tu	We	Th	Fr	Sa
			1	2	3	4
5	6	7	8	9	10	11
12	13	14	15	16	17	18
19	20	21	22	23	24	25
26	27	28	29	30	31	

August

Su	Mo	Tu	We	Th	Fr	Sa
						1
2	3	4	5	6	7	8
9	10	11	12	13	14	15
16	17	18	19	20	21	22
23	24	25	26	27	28	29
30	31					

September

Su	Mo	Tu	We	Th	Fr	Sa
		1	2	3	4	5
6	7	8	9	10	11	12
13	14	15	16	17	18	19
20	21	22	23	24	25	26
27	28	29	30			

October

Su	Mo	Tu	We	Th	Fr	Sa
				1	2	3
4	5	6	7	8	9	10
11	12	13	14	15	16	17
18	19	20	21	22	23	24
25	26	27	28	29	30	31

November

Su	Mo	Tu	We	Th	Fr	Sa
1	2	3	4	5	6	7
8	9	10	11	12	13	14
15	16	17	18	19	20	21
22	23	24	25	26	27	28
29	30					

December

Su	Mo	Tu	We	Th	Fr	Sa
		1	2	3	4	5
6	7	8	9	10	11	12
13	14	15	16	17	18	19
20	21	22	23	24	25	26
27	28	29	30	31		

GOALS 2020

GOAL	MAKE IT HAPPEN

GOAL	MAKE IT HAPPEN

GOAL	MAKE IT HAPPEN

GOALS 2020

GOAL	MAKE IT HAPPEN

GOAL	MAKE IT HAPPEN

GOAL	MAKE IT HAPPEN

HOLIDAYS 2020

Wednesday, January 1(US)	New Year's Day
Monday, January 20 (US)	Birthday of Martin Luther King, Jr.
Saturday, January 25	Chinese New Year
Friday, February 14	Valentine's Day
Monday, February 17 (US)	Washington's Birthday
Tuesday, February 25	Shrove Tuesday
Sunday, March 8	International Women's Day
Tuesday, March 17	St. Patrick's Day
Friday, April 10	Good Friday
Wednesday, April 1	April Fool's day
Sunday, April 12	Easter Sunday
Monday, April 13	Easter Monday
Tuesday, May 5	Cinco de Mayo
Friday, May 8 (UK)	May Day
Sunday, May 10	Mother's Day
Monday, May 18 (CAN)	Victoria Day
Monday, May 25 (US)	Memorial Day
Monday, May 25 (UK)	Late May Day
Sunday, June 21	Father's Day
Wednesday, July 1 (CAN)	Canada Day
Friday, July 4 (US)	Independence Day
Friday, July 14 (France)	Bastille Day
Monday, August 31 (UK)	August Bank Holiday
Monday, September 7 (US, CAN)	Labor Day
Monday, October 12 (US)	Columbus Day
Monday, October 12 (CAN)	Thanksgiving
Saturday, October 31	Halloween
Wednesday, November 11 (US)	Veterans Day
Wednesday, November 11 (CAN)	Remembrance Day
Thursday, November 26 (US)	Thanksgiving Day
Friday, December 25 (US)	Christmas Day
Saturday, December 26 (US)	Boxing Day

Some say a dog's life is easy...no worries, no taxes. I say, walk a mile in my shoes. That reminds me, I took your shoe.

SORRY, HOOMAN!

Photo

January 2020

Sun	Mon	Tue	Wed	Thu	Fri	Sat
			1	2	3	4
5	6	7	8	9	10	11
12	13	14	15	16	17	18
19	20	21	22	23	24	25
26	27	28	29	30	31	

January 2020

--- EVENTS---

--- TOP PRIORITIES---

--- VARIOUS TO DO---

--- PEOPLE TO CONNECT WITH---

--- PLACES TO VISIT---

--- THINGS FOR NEXT MONTH---

CHECKLIST-JANUARY

ITEM:	DATE:	DONE:

NOTES:

Notes…

February 2020

Sun	Mon	Tue	Wed	Thu	Fri	Sat
						1
2	3	4	5	6	7	8
9	10	11	12	13	14	15
16	17	18	19	20	21	22
23	24	25	26	27	28	29

FEBRUARY 2020

--- EVENTS---

--- TOP PRIORITIES---

--- VARIOUS TO DO---

--- PEOPLE TO CONNECT WITH---

--- PLACES TO VISIT---

--- THINGS FOR NEXT MONTH---

CHECKLIST- FEBRUARY

ITEM:	DATE:	DONE:

NOTES:

Notes...

Hello frens.
Today has been a great day
to think about my
accomplishments.
Here they are.

ZOOMIES OF THE SPEEDY VARIETY
MAXIMUM SNOOZLES
CHASING BRUCE THE SQUIRREL
BORKED AWAY ALL EVILDOERS
ATE A WORM
SPAT OUT THE WORM
SNUGGLED WITH MY
STUFFED FREN, LEROY, ON
THE HOOMAN'S BED.

March 2020

Sun	Mon	Tue	Wed	Thu	Fri	Sat
1	2	3	4	5	6	7
8	9	10	11	12	13	14
15	16	17	18	19	20	21
22	23	24	25	26	27	28
29	30	31				

MARCH 2020

--- EVENTS---	--- TOP PRIORITIES---
	--- VARIOUS TO DO---
	--- PEOPLE TO CONNECT WITH---
	--- PLACES TO VISIT---
	--- THINGS FOR NEXT MONTH---

CHECKLIST-MARCH

ITEM:	DATE:	DONE:

NOTES:

Notes…

DURING MY NIGHT TIME SNOOZLE I DREAMED THAT I DUG UP A BOX IN THE GARDEN & IT WAS FILLED WITH CHEESE

TODAY, I WILL TEST THIS OUT!

April 2020

Sun	Mon	Tue	Wed	Thu	Fri	Sat
			1	2	3	4
5	6	7	8	9	10	11
12	13	14	15	16	17	18
19	20	21	22	23	24	25
26	27	28	29	30		

APRIL 2020

--- EVENTS---

--- TOP PRIORITIES---

--- VARIOUS TO DO---

--- PEOPLE TO CONNECT WITH---

--- PLACES TO VISIT---

--- THINGS FOR NEXT MONTH---

CHECKLIST-APRIL

ITEM:	DATE:	DONE:

NOTES:

Notes…

MY EAR FLAP
IS INSIDE OUT
AND MY HOOMAN
IS NOT HOME
TO FIX IT

I HAVE GRRBORKED!
ALERT LEVEL RED

May 2020

Sun	Mon	Tue	Wed	Thu	Fri	Sat
					1	2
3	4	5	6	7	8	9
10	11	12	13	14	15	16
17	18	19	20	21	22	23
24	25	26	27	28	29	30
31						

MAY 2020

--- EVENTS---	--- TOP PRIORITIES---
	--- VARIOUS TO DO---
	--- PEOPLE TO CONNECT WITH---
	--- PLACES TO VISIT---
	--- THINGS FOR NEXT MONTH---

CHECKLIST-MAY

ITEM:	DATE:	DONE:

NOTES:

Notes…

Noise has woken me. Possible causes...
...world ending
...no other possibilities
...definite catastrophe
...wake the hooman!

NOW!

Photo

Easy Doggie Donuts

Ingredients:
1 cup flour
1 cup oats
1/3 cup coconut oil
1/2 cup peanut Butter
2 Eggs

For the topping:
Greek Yogurt
Bacon Bits

Directions:

Preheat your oven to 375 degrees. Spray a donut pan with cooking spray and set aside.

In a large bowl, combine all ingredients (except yogurt and bacon bits). You can mix with a spoon or use your hands (super fun for kids!). Mix until a dough forms. Use your hands to press the dough into the donut pan. Fill each donut cavity and press firmly to ensure everything sticks together (it won't rise, so you should make sure each space is tightly packed).

Bake in your preheated oven at 375 degrees for approximately 14 mins or until cooked completely.

Allow to cool, then carefully remove the donuts from the pan. Now you're ready to decorate them!

Set out a small bowl of plan Greek yogurt and another of bacon bits. Dip each donut carefully in the yogurt, then sprinkle with bacon bits.

Place your finished donuts in the freezer for a few moments to harden the yogurt. My dogs like to eat them straight from the freezer, but you can also store in the refrigerator. Just keep in mind that the yogurt may get a little sticky.

June 2020

Sun	Mon	Tue	Wed	Thu	Fri	Sat
	1	2	3	4	5	6
7	8	9	10	11	12	13
14	15	16	17	18	19	20
21	22	23	24	25	26	27
28	29	30				

JUNE 2020

--- EVENTS---

--- TOP PRIORITIES---

--- VARIOUS TO DO---

--- PEOPLE TO CONNECT WITH---

--- PLACES TO VISIT---

--- THINGS FOR NEXT MONTH---

CHECKLIST-JUNE

ITEM:	DATE:	DONE:

NOTES:

Notes...

The mailman left a box
at the front door
It smells like peanut butter.

I'm trying my best
to remain calm,
but I think it's for me

GRR! AWOOOOO... BOOF!

IN HAPPINESS

July 2020

Sun	Mon	Tue	Wed	Thu	Fri	Sat
			1	2	3	4
5	6	7	8	9	10	11
12	13	14	15	16	17	18
19	20	21	22	23	24	25
26	27	28	29	30	31	

JULY 2020

--- TOP PRIORITIES---

--- VARIOUS TO DO---

--- PEOPLE TO CONNECT WITH---

--- PLACES TO VISIT---

--- THINGS FOR NEXT MONTH---

CHECKLIST-JULY

ITEM:	DATE:	DONE:

NOTES:

Notes...

August 2020

Sun	Mon	Tue	Wed	Thu	Fri	Sat
						1
2	3	4	5	6	7	8
9	10	11	12	13	14	15
16	17	18	19	20	21	22
23	24	25	26	27	28	29
30	31					

AUGUST 2020

--- EVENTS---	--- TOP PRIORITIES---
	--- VARIOUS TO DO---
	--- PEOPLE TO CONNECT WITH---
	--- PLACES TO VISIT---
	--- THINGS FOR NEXT MONTH---

CHECKLIST-AUGUST

ITEM:	DATE:	DONE:

NOTES:

Notes...

Spoiled Dog Birthday Cake

Ingredients:

Cake

- 1 cup flour
- 1/2 tsp baking soda
- 1/8 cup vegetable oil
- 1/4 cup peanut butter
- 1/2 cup applesauce
- 1/2 cup pumpkin puree
- 1 egg

Frosting

- 1/2 cup plain Greek yogurt
- 1/4 cup peanut butter

Instructions:

Cake

Preheat oven to 350 degrees F.

In a large bowl, combine flour and baking soda.

In a separate bowl mix together vegetable oil, peanut butter, applesauce and pumpkin puree. Once combined, mix in egg and mix until combined.

Combine wet and dry ingredients and stir until combined.

Pour mixture into an 8" round pan (a square pan can also be used) that has been greased with oil.

Bake for approximately 25-30 minutes or until a toothpick inserted into the center comes out clean and the cake springs back when pressed lightly.

Cake
Allow to cool on a wire rack prior to removing from pan.

After cooling, add frosting if desired.

Frosting
Mix Greek yogurt and peanut butter until well combined. Spread over cake. If not serving immediately, store in refrigerator.

September 2020

Sun	Mon	Tue	Wed	Thu	Fri	Sat
		1	2	3	4	5
6	7	8	9	10	11	12
13	14	15	16	17	18	19
20	21	22	23	24	25	26
27	28	29	30			

SEPTEMBER 2020

--- EVENTS---	--- TOP PRIORITIES---
	--- VARIOUS TO DO---
	--- PEOPLE TO CONNECT WITH---
	--- PLACES TO VISIT---
	--- THINGS FOR NEXT MONTH---

CHECKLIST-SEPTEMBER

ITEM:	DATE:	DONE:

NOTES:

Notes...

THAT PESKY CAT FROM NEXT DOOR SNUCK UP ON ME WHEN I WAS HAVING A SNOOZLE ON THE COUCH.

DID ME A HECK OF A FRIGHTEN!

GRR

I'LL BE READY NEXT TIME

October 2020

Sun	Mon	Tue	Wed	Thu	Fri	Sat
				1	2	3
4	5	6	7	8	9	10
11	12	13	14	15	16	17
18	19	20	21	22	23	24
25	26	27	28	29	30	31

OCTOBER 2020

--- EVENTS---

--- TOP PRIORITIES---

--- VARIOUS TO DO---

--- PEOPLE TO CONNECT WITH---

--- PLACES TO VISIT---

--- THINGS FOR NEXT MONTH---

CHECKLIST-OCTOBER

ITEM:	DATE:	DONE:

NOTES:

Notes...

The night snoozle
is here again.
I have gathered

my stuffed frens,
Leroy & Alistair
and they are safe in
the hooman's bed.

Lorem ipsum

THEY ARE AFRAID OF THE DARK

November 2020

Sun	Mon	Tue	Wed	Thu	Fri	Sat
1	2	3	4	5	6	7
8	9	10	11	12	13	14
15	16	17	18	19	20	21
22	23	24	25	26	27	28
29	30					

NOVEMBER 2020

--- EVENTS---

--- TOP PRIORITIES---

--- VARIOUS TO DO---

--- PEOPLE TO CONNECT WITH---

--- PLACES TO VISIT---

--- THINGS FOR NEXT MONTH---

CHECKLIST-NOVEMBER

ITEM:	DATE:	DONE:

NOTES:

Notes...

I PRETENDED THAT I NEEDED TO GO THE BATHROOM

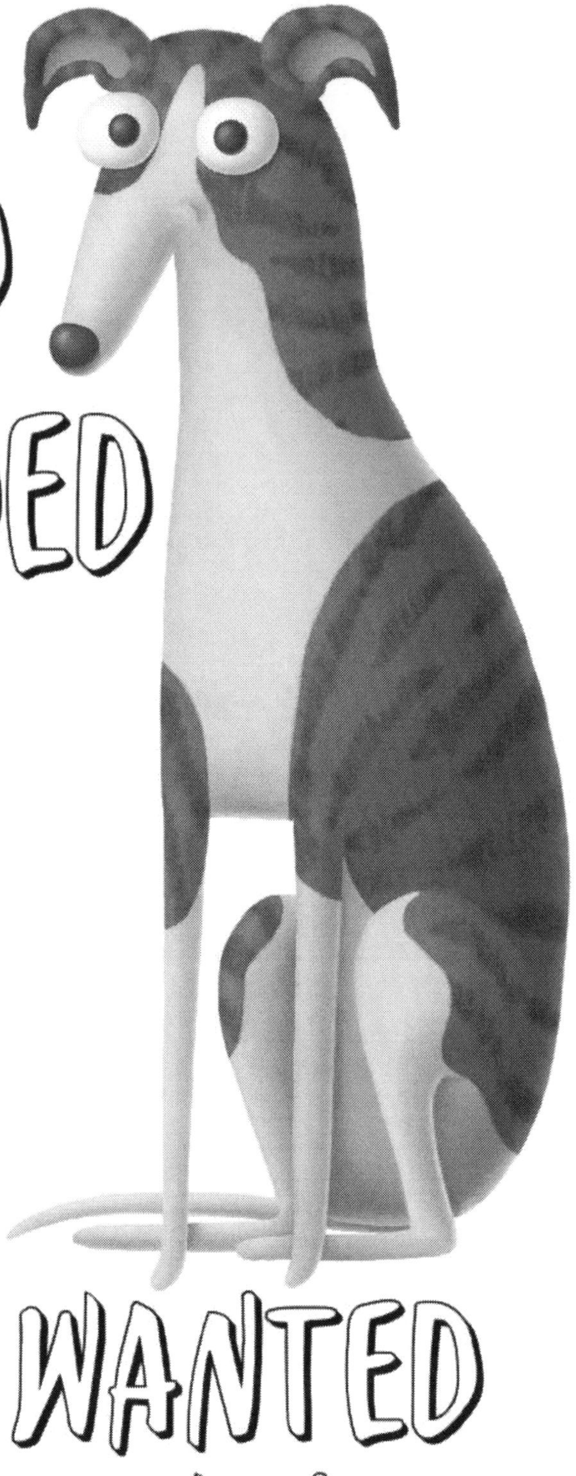

BUT I ONLY WANTED TO FEEL THE WIND ON MY NOGGIN

December 2020

Sun	Mon	Tue	Wed	Thu	Fri	Sat
		1	2	3	4	5
6	7	8	9	10	11	12
13	14	15	16	17	18	19
20	21	22	23	24	25	26
27	28	29	30	31		

DECEMBER 2020

--- EVENTS---

--- TOP PRIORITIES---

--- VARIOUS TO DO---

--- PEOPLE TO CONNECT WITH---

--- PLACES TO VISIT---

--- THINGS FOR NEXT MONTH---

CHECKLIST-DECEMBER

ITEM:	DATE:	DONE:

NOTES:

Notes…

MANY HAVE TOLD ME
WHAT A GOOD BOI I AM

AND LET'S
SAY THEY
ARE
ABSOLUTELY
RIGHT

I'D LIKE SOME CHEESE
HOOMAN

2021

January

Su	Mo	Tu	We	Th	Fr	Sa
					1	2
3	4	5	6	7	8	9
10	11	12	13	14	15	16
17	18	19	20	21	22	23
24	25	26	27	28	29	30
31						

February

Su	Mo	Tu	We	Th	Fr	Sa
	1	2	3	4	5	6
7	8	9	10	11	12	13
14	15	16	17	18	19	20
21	22	23	24	25	26	27
28						

March

Su	Mo	Tu	We	Th	Fr	Sa
	1	2	3	4	5	6
7	8	9	10	11	12	13
14	15	16	17	18	19	20
21	22	23	24	25	26	27
28	29	30	31			

April

Su	Mo	Tu	We	Th	Fr	Sa
				1	2	3
4	5	6	7	8	9	10
11	12	13	14	15	16	17
18	19	20	21	22	23	24
25	26	27	28	29	30	

May

Su	Mo	Tu	We	Th	Fr	Sa
						1
2	3	4	5	6	7	8
9	10	11	12	13	14	15
16	17	18	19	20	21	22
23	24	25	26	27	28	29
30	31					

June

Su	Mo	Tu	We	Th	Fr	Sa
		1	2	3	4	5
6	7	8	9	10	11	12
13	14	15	16	17	18	19
20	21	22	23	24	25	26
27	28	29	30			

July

Su	Mo	Tu	We	Th	Fr	Sa
				1	2	3
4	5	6	7	8	9	10
11	12	13	14	15	16	17
18	19	20	21	22	23	24
25	26	27	28	29	30	31

August

Su	Mo	Tu	We	Th	Fr	Sa
1	2	3	4	5	6	7
8	9	10	11	12	13	14
15	16	17	18	19	20	21
22	23	24	25	26	27	28
29	30	31				

September

Su	Mo	Tu	We	Th	Fr	Sa
			1	2	3	4
5	6	7	8	9	10	11
12	13	14	15	16	17	18
19	20	21	22	23	24	25
26	27	28	29	30		

October

Su	Mo	Tu	We	Th	Fr	Sa
					1	2
3	4	5	6	7	8	9
10	11	12	13	14	15	16
17	18	19	20	21	22	23
24	25	26	27	28	29	30
31						

November

Su	Mo	Tu	We	Th	Fr	Sa
	1	2	3	4	5	6
7	8	9	10	11	12	13
14	15	16	17	18	19	20
21	22	23	24	25	26	27
28	29	30				

December

Su	Mo	Tu	We	Th	Fr	Sa
			1	2	3	4
5	6	7	8	9	10	11
12	13	14	15	16	17	18
19	20	21	22	23	24	25
26	27	28	29	30	31	

GOALS 2021

GOAL	MAKE IT HAPPEN

GOAL	MAKE IT HAPPEN

GOAL	MAKE IT HAPPEN

GOALS 2021

GOAL	MAKE IT HAPPEN

GOAL	MAKE IT HAPPEN

GOAL	MAKE IT HAPPEN

HOLIDAYS 2021

Friday, January 1	New Year's Day
Monday, January 18	Birthday of Martin Luther King, Jr.
Saturday, Feb 2	Groundhog Day
Friday, Feb 12	Chinese New Year
Sunday, Feb 14	Valentine's Day
Monday, Feb 18	Washington's Birthday
Monday, March 8 (UK/CAN)	Commonwealth Day
Wednesday, March 17	St. Patrick's Day
Sunday, March 14 (UK)	Mother's Day
Friday, April 2	Good Friday
Sunday, April 4	Easter Sunday
Monday, April 5	Easter Monday
Wednesday, April 21	Queen's Birthday
Sunday, May 5	Cinco de Mayo
Saturday, May 1	May Day
Monday, May 3 (UK)	Early May Bank Holiday
Sunday, May 9 (US/CAN)	Mother's Day
Monday, May 24 (CAN)	Victoria Day
Monday, May 31 (UK)	Spring Bank Holiday
Monday, May 27 (US)	Memorial Day
Sunday, June 20 (US/UK/CAN)	Father's Day
Thursday, July 1	Canada Day
Sunday, July 4	Independence Day
Sunday, July 14	Bastille Day
Monday, September 6 (US/CAN)	Labour Day
Monday, Oct 11	Columbus Day Thanksgiving (CAN)
Sunday, Oct 31	Halloween
Thursday, Nov 11 (US/UK)	Veteran's Day Remembrance Day
Friday, Nov 5 (UK)	Guy Fawkes Night
Thursday, Nov 25	Thanksgiving Day
Saturday, Dec 25	Christmas Day
Sunday, Dec 26	Boxing Day
Friday, Dec 31	New Year's Eve

A new month is upon us....
or so the hooman tells me.
Hooman time constructs do me a
bamboozle. I prefer to break it down
into snoozes, non snoozes and........
MAXIMUM BORKDRIVE

Photo

January 2021

Sun	Mon	Tue	Wed	Thu	Fri	Sat
					1	2
3	4	5	6	7	8	9
10	11	12	13	14	15	16
17	18	19	20	21	22	23
24	25	26	27	28	29	30
31						

JANUARY 2021

--- EVENTS---	--- TOP PRIORITIES---
	--- VARIOUS TO DO---
	--- PEOPLE TO CONNECT WITH---
	--- PLACES TO VISIT---
	--- THINGS FOR NEXT MONTH---

CHECKLIST-JANUARY

ITEM:	DATE:	DONE:

NOTES:

Notes...

February 2021

Sun	Mon	Tue	Wed	Thu	Fri	Sat
	1	2	3	4	5	6
7	8	9	10	11	12	13
14	15	16	17	18	19	20
21	22	23	24	25	26	27
28						

FEBRUARY 2021

--- EVENTS---

--- TOP PRIORITIES---

--- VARIOUS TO DO---

--- PEOPLE TO CONNECT WITH---

--- PLACES TO VISIT---

--- THINGS FOR NEXT MONTH---

CHECKLIST-FEBRUARY

ITEM:	DATE:	DONE:

NOTES:

Notes…

I HAVE TWO SPEEDS FOR WALKING

FASTER THAN YOU & COMPLETELY IMMOBILE (DRAGGING SPEED)

OF COURSE SOME PEANUT BUTTER OR A GOOD STICK COULD CHANGE THAT!

March 2021

Sun	Mon	Tue	Wed	Thu	Fri	Sat
	1	2	3	4	5	6
7	8	9	10	11	12	13
14	15	16	17	18	19	20
21	22	23	24	25	26	27
28	29	30	31			

MARCH 2021

--- EVENTS---	--- TOP PRIORITIES---
	--- VARIOUS TO DO---
	--- PEOPLE TO CONNECT WITH---
	--- PLACES TO VISIT---
	--- THINGS FOR NEXT MONTH---

CHECKLIST-MARCH

ITEM:	DATE:	DONE:

NOTES:

Notes...

April 2021

Sun	Mon	Tue	Wed	Thu	Fri	Sat
				1	2	3
4	5	6	7	8	9	10
11	12	13	14	15	16	17
18	19	20	21	22	23	24
25	26	27	28	29	30	

APRIL 2021

--- EVENTS---

--- TOP PRIORITIES---

--- VARIOUS TO DO---

--- PEOPLE TO CONNECT WITH---

--- PLACES TO VISIT---

--- THINGS FOR NEXT MONTH---

CHECKLIST-APRIL

ITEM:	DATE:	DONE:

NOTES:

Notes…

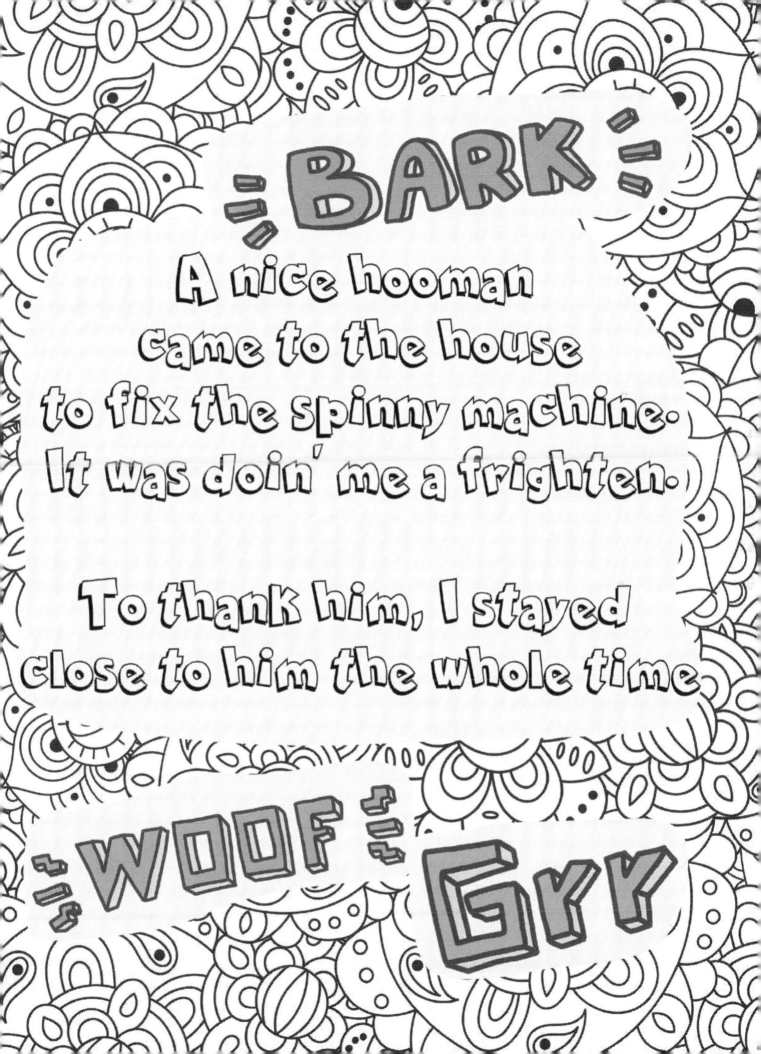

May 2021

Sun	Mon	Tue	Wed	Thu	Fri	Sat
						1
2	3	4	5	6	7	8
9	10	11	12	13	14	15
16	17	18	19	20	21	22
23	24	25	26	27	28	29
30	31					

MAY 2021

--- EVENTS---	--- TOP PRIORITIES---
	--- VARIOUS TO DO---
	--- PEOPLE TO CONNECT WITH---
	--- PLACES TO VISIT---
	--- THINGS FOR NEXT MONTH---

CHECKLIST-MAY

ITEM:	DATE:	DONE:

NOTES:

Notes…

MY HOOMAN IS HOSTING
A DINNER PARTY TONIGHT

AND it's MY joB to
GReet ALL tHe Guests

CALMLY ... NO JUMPING!!!

THIS IS NOT POSSIBLE

I SHALL SEEK THE HELP OF
MY STUFFED FREN,
CHRISTMAS TURKEY

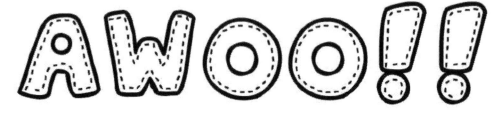
AWOO!!!

Guys, I just had a morning walk. Some big doggo borked at me and I almost caught Bruce, the lizard.

LIFE IS GOOD!

Photo

Bacon & Peanut Butter Glaze

Ingredients:

Dog biscuits:
- 1 cup pumpkin
- 1/2 cup peanut butter
- 2 eggs
- 1/4 cup oil
- 2 1/2 cups whole wheat flour
- 1 teaspoon baking soda

Glaze:
- 2 tablespoons bacon grease, coconut oil, chicken fat, or any other fat that will solidify at room temperature, melted
- 1/4 cup smooth peanut butter

Instructions:

Preheat oven to 350 degrees.

Combine pumpkin, peanut butter, eggs, and oil in a bowl. Add in baking soda and whole wheat flour. Stir until a stiff dough forms. Knead dough or mix just until flour is incorporated.

Roll out dough with a rolling pin and use a cookie cutter to cut out dog bone shapes, or just bake into little circles like cookies. Bake for 15 minutes.

Whisk the bacon grease and peanut butter until very smooth. Drizzle over the treats and cool till glaze hardens (it does best in the fridge or freezer).

Please check with your vet or use an alternative type of oil if you are concerned about bacon grease.

June 2021

Sun	Mon	Tue	Wed	Thu	Fri	Sat
		1	2	3	4	5
6	7	8	9	10	11	12
13	14	15	16	17	18	19
20	21	22	23	24	25	26
27	28	29	30			

JUNE 2021

--- EVENTS---	--- TOP PRIORITIES---
	--- VARIOUS TO DO---
	--- PEOPLE TO CONNECT WITH---
	--- PLACES TO VISIT---
	--- THINGS FOR NEXT MONTH---

CHECKLIST-JUNE

ITEM:	DATE:	DONE:

NOTES:

Notes...

July 2021

Sun	Mon	Tue	Wed	Thu	Fri	Sat
				1	2	3
4	5	6	7	8	9	10
11	12	13	14	15	16	17
18	19	20	21	22	23	24
25	26	27	28	29	30	31

JULY 2021

--- EVENTS---	--- TOP PRIORITIES---
	--- VARIOUS TO DO---
	--- PEOPLE TO CONNECT WITH---
	--- PLACES TO VISIT---
	--- THINGS FOR NEXT MONTH---

CHECKLIST-JULY

ITEM:	DATE:	DONE:

NOTES:

Notes...

SOMETHING HAS WOKEN ME UP

IT'S THAT PESKY CAT, BORIS

I HAVE GATHERED
MY STUFFED FREN,
ALISTAIR THE CROCODILE
AND PREPARED
FOR EXTENDED SNOOZLES

August 2021

Sun	Mon	Tue	Wed	Thu	Fri	Sat
1	2	3	4	5	6	7
8	9	10	11	12	13	14
15	16	17	18	19	20	21
22	23	24	25	26	27	28
29	30	31				

AUGUST 2021

--- EVENTS---	--- TOP PRIORITIES---
	--- VARIOUS TO DO---
	--- PEOPLE TO CONNECT WITH---
	--- PLACES TO VISIT---
	--- THINGS FOR NEXT MONTH---

CHECKLIST-AUGUST

ITEM:	DATE:	DONE:

NOTES:

Notes...

September 2021

Sun	Mon	Tue	Wed	Thu	Fri	Sat
			1	2	3	4
5	6	7	8	9	10	11
12	13	14	15	16	17	18
19	20	21	22	23	24	25
26	27	28	29	30		

SEPTEMBER 2021

--- EVENTS---	--- TOP PRIORITIES---
	--- VARIOUS TO DO---
	--- PEOPLE TO CONNECT WITH---
	--- PLACES TO VISIT---
	--- THINGS FOR NEXT MONTH---

CHECKLIST-SEPTEMBER

ITEM:	DATE:	DONE:

NOTES:

Notes…

LET ME TELL YOU ABOUT MY BEST STUFFED FREN, JEREMY

HE'S MY BESTEST PAL

HE'S GOT A LONG SNOOT FLOPPY EAR FLAPS

HE AGREES WITH EVERYTHING I SAY

October 2021

Sun	Mon	Tue	Wed	Thu	Fri	Sat
					1	2
3	4	5	6	7	8	9
10	11	12	13	14	15	16
17	18	19	20	21	22	23
24	25	26	27	28	29	30
31						

OCTOBER 2021

--- EVENTS---

--- TOP PRIORITIES---

--- VARIOUS TO DO---

--- PEOPLE TO CONNECT WITH---

--- PLACES TO VISIT---

--- THINGS FOR NEXT MONTH---

CHECKLIST-OCTOBER

ITEM:	DATE:	DONE:

NOTES:

Notes…

MY HOOMAN HAS BOUGHT A NEW SOFA AND I'M NOT ALLOWED TO SNOOZLE ON IT.

I HAVE NO IDEA WHY BUT THIS SHALL BE REMEDIED

I WILL SLOWLY CLIMB UP ONE PAW AT A TIME.

NO ONE WILL EVER NOTICE!

November 2021

Sun	Mon	Tue	Wed	Thu	Fri	Sat
	1	2	3	4	5	6
7	8	9	10	11	12	13
14	15	16	17	18	19	20
21	22	23	24	25	26	27
28	29	30				

NOVEMBER 2021

--- EVENTS---

--- TOP PRIORITIES---

--- VARIOUS TO DO---

--- PEOPLE TO CONNECT WITH---

--- PLACES TO VISIT---

--- THINGS FOR NEXT MONTH---

CHECKLIST-NOVEMBER

ITEM:	DATE:	DONE:

NOTES:

Notes…

Cranberry Cookies

- **Ingredients:**
- 2 eggs
- 1.5 cups almond flour
- 1 Tablespoon coconut oil
- 3-4 Tablespoons coconut flour
- 1/2 cup dried cranberries

Instructions:

Preheat oven to 325 degrees.

Beat the eggs and set aside.

Combine almond flour, coconut oil, and dried cranberries in a bowl.

Add in the eggs and knead the ingredients with your hands. Dough will be wet and sticky.

Add in the coconut flour one tablespoon at a time to achieve a consistency that is easy to roll out and not overly sticky. This should take approximately 3-4 TBSP.

Roll out the dough and cut out the treats using heart shaped cookie cutters. Place the treats on a cookie sheet lined with parchment paper.

Bake for 15-18 minutes or until crisp.

December 2021

Sun	Mon	Tue	Wed	Thu	Fri	Sat
			1	2	3	4
5	6	7	8	9	10	11
12	13	14	15	16	17	18
19	20	21	22	23	24	25
26	27	28	29	30	31	

DECEMBER 2021

--- EVENTS---	--- TOP PRIORITIES---
	--- VARIOUS TO DO---
	--- PEOPLE TO CONNECT WITH---
	--- PLACES TO VISIT---
	--- THINGS FOR NEXT MONTH---

CHECKLIST-DECEMBER

ITEM:	DATE:	DONE:

NOTES:

Notes…

A LOT HAPPENED ON OUR MORNING WALK

I found a perfectly good chimkin leg in the neighbor's trash, but the hooman wouldn't let me have it.

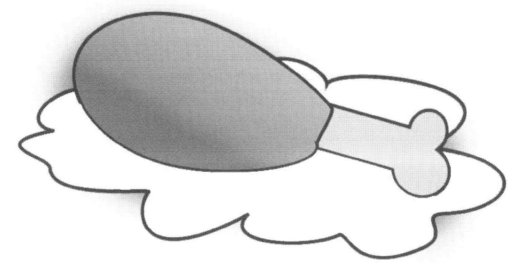

THERE WAS ALSO A VERY SCARY PLASTIC BAG

2022

January

Su	Mo	Tu	We	Th	Fr	Sa
						1
2	3	4	5	6	7	8
9	10	11	12	13	14	15
16	17	18	19	20	21	22
23	24	25	26	27	28	29
30	31					

February

Su	Mo	Tu	We	Th	Fr	Sa
		1	2	3	4	5
6	7	8	9	10	11	12
13	14	15	16	17	18	19
20	21	22	23	24	25	26
27	28					

March

Su	Mo	Tu	We	Th	Fr	Sa
		1	2	3	4	5
6	7	8	9	10	11	12
13	14	15	16	17	18	19
20	21	22	23	24	25	26
27	28	29	30	31		

April

Su	Mo	Tu	We	Th	Fr	Sa
					1	2
3	4	5	6	7	8	9
10	11	12	13	14	15	16
17	18	19	20	21	22	23
24	25	26	27	28	29	30

May

Su	Mo	Tu	We	Th	Fr	Sa
1	2	3	4	5	6	7
8	9	10	11	12	13	14
15	16	17	18	19	20	21
22	23	24	25	26	27	28
29	30	31				

June

Su	Mo	Tu	We	Th	Fr	Sa
			1	2	3	4
5	6	7	8	9	10	11
12	13	14	15	16	17	18
19	20	21	22	23	24	25
26	27	28	29	30		

July

Su	Mo	Tu	We	Th	Fr	Sa
					1	2
3	4	5	6	7	8	9
10	11	12	13	14	15	16
17	18	19	20	21	22	23
24	25	26	27	28	29	30
31						

August

Su	Mo	Tu	We	Th	Fr	Sa
	1	2	3	4	5	6
7	8	9	10	11	12	13
14	15	16	17	18	19	20
21	22	23	24	25	26	27
28	29	30	31			

September

Su	Mo	Tu	We	Th	Fr	Sa
				1	2	3
4	5	6	7	8	9	10
11	12	13	14	15	16	17
18	19	20	21	22	23	24
25	26	27	28	29	30	

October

Su	Mo	Tu	We	Th	Fr	Sa
						1
2	3	4	5	6	7	8
9	10	11	12	13	14	15
16	17	18	19	20	21	22
23	24	25	26	27	28	29
30	31					

November

Su	Mo	Tu	We	Th	Fr	Sa
		1	2	3	4	5
6	7	8	9	10	11	12
13	14	15	16	17	18	19
20	21	22	23	24	25	26
27	28	29	30			

December

Su	Mo	Tu	We	Th	Fr	Sa
				1	2	3
4	5	6	7	8	9	10
11	12	13	14	15	16	17
18	19	20	21	22	23	24
25	26	27	28	29	30	31

GOALS 2022

GOAL	MAKE IT HAPPEN

GOAL	MAKE IT HAPPEN

GOAL	MAKE IT HAPPEN

GOALS 2022

GOAL	MAKE IT HAPPEN

GOAL	MAKE IT HAPPEN

GOAL	MAKE IT HAPPEN

HOLIDAYS 2022

Saturday, January 1	New Year's Day
Monday, January 17	Birthday of Martin Luther King, Jr.
Saturday, Feb 2	Groundhog Day
Wednesday, Feb 2	Chinese New Year
Monday, Feb 14	Valentine's Day
Monday, Feb 21	Washington's Birthday
Monday, March 14 (UK/CAN)	Commonwealth Day
Thursday, March 17	St. Patrick's Day
Thursday, March 31 (UK)	Mother's Day
Friday, April 15	Good Friday
Sunday, April 17	Easter Sunday
Monday, April 18	Easter Monday
Thursday, April 21	Queen's Birthday
Sunday, May 5	Cinco de Mayo
Sunday, May 1	May Day
Monday, May 2 (UK)	Early May Bank Holiday
Sunday, May 8 (US/CAN)	Mother's Day
Monday, May 23 (CAN)	Victoria Day
Monday, May 30 (UK)	Spring Bank Holiday
Monday, May 30 (US)	Memorial Day
Sunday, June 19 (UK/US/CAN)	Father's Day
Friday, July 1	Canada Day
Monday, July 4	Independence Day
Thursday, July 14	Bastille Day
Monday, September 5 (US/CAN)	Labour Day
Monday, Oct 10	Columbus Day Thanksgiving (CAN)
Monday, Oct 31	Halloween
Friday, Nov 11 (US/UK)	Veteran's Day Remembrance Day
Saturday, Nov 5 (UK)	Guy Fawkes Night
Thursday, Nov 25	Thanksgiving Day
Sunday, Dec 25	Christmas Day
Monday, Dec 26	Boxing Day
Saturday, Dec 31	New Year's Eve

I have been programming my hooman. Every time he gives me food, I bork. Eventually, every time I bork, he will give me food.

I WANT CHEESE!

Photo

January 2022

Sun	Mon	Tue	Wed	Thu	Fri	Sat
						1
2	3	4	5	6	7	8
9	10	11	12	13	14	15
16	17	18	19	20	21	22
23	24	25	26	27	28	29
30	31					

JANUARY 2022

--- EVENTS---

--- TOP PRIORITIES---

--- VARIOUS TO DO---

--- PEOPLE TO CONNECT WITH---

--- PLACES TO VISIT---

--- THINGS FOR NEXT MONTH---

CHECKLIST-JANUARY

ITEM:	DATE:	DONE:

NOTES:

Notes…

THE HOOMAN BELIEVES HE HAS LOST HIS SOCKS IN THE SPINNY MACHINE

I BEG TO DIFFER

I steal them way before that

February 2022

Sun	Mon	Tue	Wed	Thu	Fri	Sat
		1	2	3	4	5
6	7	8	9	10	11	12
13	14	15	16	17	18	19
20	21	22	23	24	25	26
27	28					

FEBRUARY 2022

--- EVENTS---

--- TOP PRIORITIES---

--- VARIOUS TO DO---

--- PEOPLE TO CONNECT WITH---

--- PLACES TO VISIT---

--- THINGS FOR NEXT MONTH---

CHECKLIST-FEBRUARY

ITEM:	DATE:	DONE:

NOTES:

Notes…

I HEAR A DOGGO BORKING IN THE DISTANCE

It is my duty to respond so that all the other doggos know I heard the initial borking

IT'S JUST GOOD MANNERS!

: WOOF :

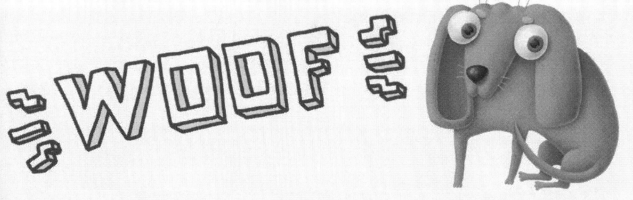

March 2022

Sun	Mon	Tue	Wed	Thu	Fri	Sat
		1	2	3	4	5
6	7	8	9	10	11	12
13	14	15	16	17	18	19
20	21	22	23	24	25	26
27	28	29	30	31		

MARCH 2022

--- EVENTS---

--- TOP PRIORITIES---

--- VARIOUS TO DO---

--- PEOPLE TO CONNECT WITH---

--- PLACES TO VISIT---

--- THINGS FOR NEXT MONTH---

CHECKLIST-MARCH

ITEM:	DATE:	DONE:

NOTES:

Notes...

April 2022

Sun	Mon	Tue	Wed	Thu	Fri	Sat
					1	2
3	4	5	6	7	8	9
10	11	12	13	14	15	16
17	18	19	20	21	22	23
24	25	26	27	28	29	30

APRIL 2022

--- EVENTS---

--- TOP PRIORITIES---

--- VARIOUS TO DO---

--- PEOPLE TO CONNECT WITH---

--- PLACES TO VISIT---

--- THINGS FOR NEXT MONTH---

CHECKLIST-APRIL

ITEM:	DATE:	DONE:

NOTES:

Notes…

We have new neighbors & they have a new pupper

I AM SO EXCITED!!

I shall take my stuffed fren, Leroy to make frens

MY TAILS A WAGGIN'

May 2022

Sun	Mon	Tue	Wed	Thu	Fri	Sat
1	2	3	4	5	6	7
8	9	10	11	12	13	14
15	16	17	18	19	20	21
22	23	24	25	26	27	28
29	30	31				

MAY 2022

--- EVENTS---

--- TOP PRIORITIES---

--- VARIOUS TO DO---

--- PEOPLE TO CONNECT WITH---

--- PLACES TO VISIT---

--- THINGS FOR NEXT MONTH---

CHECKLIST-MAY

ITEM:	DATE:	DONE:

NOTES:

Notes…

I HAVE NO PLANS
TODAY
JUST SNOOZLES
AND SNACKS

I CANCELLED MY PLANS
WITH MY FLOOFER
FREN, TIMBO
ABOUT HOW TO DO

MAXIMUM
ZOOMIES

ON HARD WOOD
FLOORS

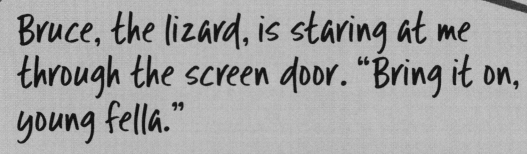

Bruce, the lizard, is staring at me through the screen door. "Bring it on, young fella."

DOIN' ME A FRIGHTEN!

Photo

Spinach, Carrot & Zucchini Treats

Ingredients:

- 1 cup pumpkin puree
- 1/4 cup peanut butter
- 2 large eggs
- 1/2 cup old fashioned oats
- 3 cups whole wheat flour, or more, as needed
- 1 carrot, peeled and shredded
- 1 zucchini, shredded
- 1 cup baby spinach, chopped

Instructions:

Preheat oven to 350 degrees F. Line a baking sheet with parchment paper or a silicone baking mat; set aside.

In the bowl of an electric mixer fitted with the paddle attachment, beat pumpkin puree, peanut butter and eggs on medium-high until well combined, about 1-2 minutes.

Gradually add old fashioned oats and 2 1/2 cups flour at low speed, beating just until incorporated. Add an additional 1/4 cup flour at a time just until the dough is no longer sticky. Add carrot, zucchini and spinach, beating just until incorporated.

Working on a lightly floured surface, knead the dough 3-4 times until it comes together. Using a rolling pin, roll the dough to 1/4-inch thickness. Using cookie cutters, cut out desired shapes and place onto the prepared baking sheet.

Place into oven and bake until the edges are golden brown, about 20-25 minutes. Let cool completely.

June 2022

Sun	Mon	Tue	Wed	Thu	Fri	Sat
			1	2	3	4
5	6	7	8	9	10	11
12	13	14	15	16	17	18
19	20	21	22	23	24	25
26	27	28	29	30		

JUNE 2022

--- EVENTS---

--- TOP PRIORITIES---

--- VARIOUS TO DO---

--- PEOPLE TO CONNECT WITH---

--- PLACES TO VISIT---

--- THINGS FOR NEXT MONTH---

CHECKLIST-JUNE

ITEM:	DATE:	DONE:

NOTES:

Notes…

I HAVE MISPLACED MY NEW FREN, CHRISTMAS TURKEY

ALERT LEVEL RED

NEVER MIND I WAS LYING ON HIM THE WHOLE TIME

ALERT LEVEL GREEN

July 2022

Sun	Mon	Tue	Wed	Thu	Fri	Sat
					1	2
3	4	5	6	7	8	9
10	11	12	13	14	15	16
17	18	19	20	21	22	23
24	25	26	27	28	29	30
31						

JULY 2022

--- EVENTS---	--- TOP PRIORITIES---
	--- VARIOUS TO DO---
	--- PEOPLE TO CONNECT WITH---
	--- PLACES TO VISIT---
	--- THINGS FOR NEXT MONTH---

JULY 2022

CHECKLIST-JULY

ITEM:	DATE:	DONE:

NOTES:

Notes…

August 2022

Sun	Mon	Tue	Wed	Thu	Fri	Sat
	1	2	3	4	5	6
7	8	9	10	11	12	13
14	15	16	17	18	19	20
21	22	23	24	25	26	27
28	29	30	31			

AUGUST 2022

--- EVENTS---

--- TOP PRIORITIES---

--- VARIOUS TO DO---

--- PEOPLE TO CONNECT WITH---

--- PLACES TO VISIT---

--- THINGS FOR NEXT MONTH---

CHECKLIST-AUGUST

ITEM:	DATE:	DONE:

NOTES:

Notes…

SOMETIMES, MY HOOMAN WILL LIFT UP MY EAR FLAP AND SCRATCH MY NOGGIN

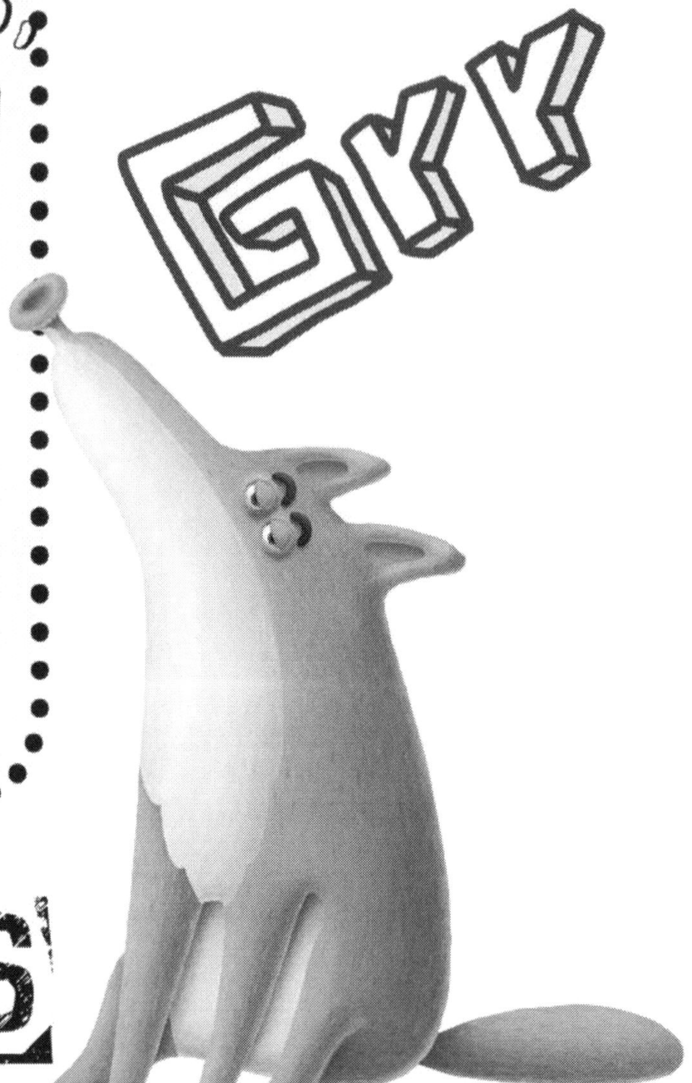

THIS IS COMPLETELY UNNECESSARY

September 2022

Sun	Mon	Tue	Wed	Thu	Fri	Sat
				1	2	3
4	5	6	7	8	9	10
11	12	13	14	15	16	17
18	19	20	21	22	23	24
25	26	27	28	29	30	

SEPTEMBER 2022

--- EVENTS---

--- TOP PRIORITIES---

--- VARIOUS TO DO---

--- PEOPLE TO CONNECT WITH---

--- PLACES TO VISIT---

--- THINGS FOR NEXT MONTH---

CHECKLIST-SEPTEMBER

ITEM:	DATE:	DONE:

NOTES:

Notes…

I JUST WOKE UP
FROM MY AFTERNOON
POWER SNOOZLE

WHICH IS AFTER THE
MORNING SNOOZLE

AND BEFORE MY
NIGHT TIME SNOOZLE

I CAN'T KEEP UP WITH MY DAY!

October 2022

Sun	Mon	Tue	Wed	Thu	Fri	Sat
						1
2	3	4	5	6	7	8
9	10	11	12	13	14	15
16	17	18	19	20	21	22
23	24	25	26	27	28	29
30	31					

OCTOBER 2022

--- EVENTS---	--- TOP PRIORITIES---
	--- VARIOUS TO DO---
	--- PEOPLE TO CONNECT WITH---
	--- PLACES TO VISIT---
	--- THINGS FOR NEXT MONTH---

CHECKLIST-OCTOBER

ITEM:	DATE:	DONE:

NOTES:

Notes…

IF YOU HEAR A SINGLE **BORK** AND THEN A **BOOF**

IT'S ONLY ME TESTING THE SAFETY OF THE HOUSEHOLD

other doggos may respond & then we have a chorus!

November 2022

Sun	Mon	Tue	Wed	Thu	Fri	Sat
		1	2	3	4	5
6	7	8	9	10	11	12
13	14	15	16	17	18	19
20	21	22	23	24	25	26
27	28	29	30			

NOVEMBER 2022

--- EVENTS---	--- TOP PRIORITIES---
	--- VARIOUS TO DO---
	--- PEOPLE TO CONNECT WITH---
	--- PLACES TO VISIT---
	--- THINGS FOR NEXT MONTH---

CHECKLIST-NOVEMBER

ITEM:	DATE:	DONE:

NOTES:

Notes…

DURING MY NIGHT TIME SNOOZLE I DREAMED THAT I DUG UP A BOX IN THE GARDEN & IT WAS FILLED WITH CHEESE

TODAY, I WILL TEST THIS OUT!

Bacon Cheddar Treats

Ingredients:

- 1 ½ cups rolled oats
- ½ cup shredded cheddar cheese
- 4 strips bacon, cooked and crumbled
- 2 eggs

Instructions:

Preheat oven to 350 degrees Fahrenheit.

Add oats, cheese, and bacon to the bowl of a food processor and process until ingredients reach a crumb-like consistency.

Add two eggs to food processor and process until mixture resembles a sticky dough.

Sprinkle flour or finely ground oats onto a wood cutting board and roll out dough to about ¼-inch thick. Using a cookie cutter, cut out dough into desired shape.

Transfer dog treats to a parchment-lined baking sheet and cook for 20 minutes.

Cool treats completely and store in an airtight glass or plastic container.

December 2022

Sun	Mon	Tue	Wed	Thu	Fri	Sat
				1	2	3
4	5	6	7	8	9	10
11	12	13	14	15	16	17
18	19	20	21	22	23	24
25	26	27	28	29	30	31

DECEMBER 2022

--- EVENTS---

--- TOP PRIORITIES---

--- VARIOUS TO DO---

--- PEOPLE TO CONNECT WITH---

--- PLACES TO VISIT---

--- THINGS FOR NEXT MONTH---

CHECKLIST-DECEMBER

ITEM:	DATE:	DONE:

NOTES:

Notes…

2023

January

Su	Mo	Tu	We	Th	Fr	Sa
1	2	3	4	5	6	7
8	9	10	11	12	13	14
15	16	17	18	19	20	21
22	23	24	25	26	27	28
29	30	31				

February

Su	Mo	Tu	We	Th	Fr	Sa
			1	2	3	4
5	6	7	8	9	10	11
12	13	14	15	16	17	18
19	20	21	22	23	24	25
26	27	28				

March

Su	Mo	Tu	We	Th	Fr	Sa
			1	2	3	4
5	6	7	8	9	10	11
12	13	14	15	16	17	18
19	20	21	22	23	24	25
26	27	28	29	30	31	

April

Su	Mo	Tu	We	Th	Fr	Sa
						1
2	3	4	5	6	7	8
9	10	11	12	13	14	15
16	17	18	19	20	21	22
23	24	25	26	27	28	29
30						

May

Su	Mo	Tu	We	Th	Fr	Sa
	1	2	3	4	5	6
7	8	9	10	11	12	13
14	15	16	17	18	19	20
21	22	23	24	25	26	27
28	29	30	31			

June

Su	Mo	Tu	We	Th	Fr	Sa
				1	2	3
4	5	6	7	8	9	10
11	12	13	14	15	16	17
18	19	20	21	22	23	24
25	26	27	28	29	30	

July

Su	Mo	Tu	We	Th	Fr	Sa
						1
2	3	4	5	6	7	8
9	10	11	12	13	14	15
16	17	18	19	20	21	22
23	24	25	26	27	28	29
30	31					

August

Su	Mo	Tu	We	Th	Fr	Sa
		1	2	3	4	5
6	7	8	9	10	11	12
13	14	15	16	17	18	19
20	21	22	23	24	25	26
27	28	29	30	31		

September

Su	Mo	Tu	We	Th	Fr	Sa
					1	2
3	4	5	6	7	8	9
10	11	12	13	14	15	16
17	18	19	20	21	22	23
24	25	26	27	28	29	30

October

Su	Mo	Tu	We	Th	Fr	Sa
1	2	3	4	5	6	7
8	9	10	11	12	13	14
15	16	17	18	19	20	21
22	23	24	25	26	27	28
29	30	31				

November

Su	Mo	Tu	We	Th	Fr	Sa
			1	2	3	4
5	6	7	8	9	10	11
12	13	14	15	16	17	18
19	20	21	22	23	24	25
26	27	28	29	30		

December

Su	Mo	Tu	We	Th	Fr	Sa
					1	2
3	4	5	6	7	8	9
10	11	12	13	14	15	16
17	18	19	20	21	22	23
24	25	26	27	28	29	30
31						

GOALS 2023

GOAL	MAKE IT HAPPEN

GOAL	MAKE IT HAPPEN

GOAL	MAKE IT HAPPEN

GOALS 2023

GOAL	MAKE IT HAPPEN

GOAL	MAKE IT HAPPEN

GOAL	MAKE IT HAPPEN

HOLIDAYS 2023

Sunday, January 1	New Year's Day
Monday, January 16	Birthday of Martin Luther King, Jr.
Thursday, Feb 2	Groundhog Day
Sunday, Jan 22	Chinese New Year
Tuesday, Feb 14	Valentine's Day
Monday, Feb 20	Washington's Birthday
Monday, March 13 (UK/CAN)	Commonwealth Day
Friday, March 17	St. Patrick's Day
Thursday, March 19 (UK)	Mother's Day
Friday, April 7	Good Friday
Sunday, April 9	Easter Sunday
Monday, April 10	Easter Monday
Friday, April 21	Queen's Birthday
Friday, May 5	Cinco de Mayo
Monday, May 1	May Day
Monday, May 1 (UK)	Early May Bank Holiday
Sunday, May 14 (US/CAN)	Mother's Day
Monday, May 22 (CAN)	Victoria Day
Monday, May 29 (UK)	Spring Bank Holiday
Monday, May 29 (US)	Memorial Day
Sunday, June 18 (UK/US/CAN)	Father's Day
Monday, July 1	Canada Day
Tuesday, July 4	Independence Day
Friday, July 14	Bastille Day
Monday, September 4 (US/CAN)	Labor Day
Monday, Oct 9	Columbus Day Thanksgiving (CAN)
Tuesday, Oct 31	Halloween
Saturday, Nov 11 (US/UK)	Veteran's Day Remembrance Day
Sunday, Nov 5 (UK)	Guy Fawkes Night
Thursday, Nov 23	Thanksgiving Day
Monday, Dec 25	Christmas Day
Tuesday, Dec 26	Boxing Day
Sunday, Dec 31	New Year's Eve

The hooman gave me an extra long hug and direct eye contact. These are heckin' signals. We're on the same page.

I FEEL CHIMKIN COMING!

Photo

January 2023

Sun	Mon	Tue	Wed	Thu	Fri	Sat
1	2	3	4	5	6	7
8	9	10	11	12	13	14
15	16	17	18	19	20	21
22	23	24	25	26	27	28
29	30	31				

JANUARY 2023

--- EVENTS---	--- TOP PRIORITIES---
	--- VARIOUS TO DO---
	--- PEOPLE TO CONNECT WITH---
	--- PLACES TO VISIT---
	--- THINGS FOR NEXT MONTH---

CHECKLIST-JANUARY

ITEM:	DATE:	DONE:

NOTES:

Notes…

Today, I did a
zoom so speedy
my ear flaps flew
back

MY FLOOFER FREN FROM
NEXT DOOR WAS
WELL-IMPRESSED!

February 2023

Sun	Mon	Tue	Wed	Thu	Fri	Sat
			1	2	3	4
5	6	7	8	9	10	11
12	13	14	15	16	17	18
19	20	21	22	23	24	25
26	27	28				

FEBRUARY 2023

--- EVENTS---

--- TOP PRIORITIES---

--- VARIOUS TO DO---

--- PEOPLE TO CONNECT WITH---

--- PLACES TO VISIT---

--- THINGS FOR NEXT MONTH---

CHECKLIST-FEBRUARY

ITEM:	DATE:	DONE:

NOTES:

Notes…

March 2023

Sun	Mon	Tue	Wed	Thu	Fri	Sat
			1	2	3	4
5	6	7	8	9	10	11
12	13	14	15	16	17	18
19	20	21	22	23	24	25
26	27	28	29	30	31	

MARCH 2023

--- EVENTS---

--- TOP PRIORITIES---

--- VARIOUS TO DO---

--- PEOPLE TO CONNECT WITH---

--- PLACES TO VISIT---

--- THINGS FOR NEXT MONTH---

CHECKLIST-MARCH

ITEM:	DATE:	DONE:

NOTES:

Notes…

I ACCIDENTALLY STOLE THE TOILET PAPER AND DECORATED THE WHOLE HOUSE

MY HOOMAN WAS WELL PLEASED !

April 2023

Sun	Mon	Tue	Wed	Thu	Fri	Sat
						1
2	3	4	5	6	7	8
9	10	11	12	13	14	15
16	17	18	19	20	21	22
23	24	25	26	27	28	29
30						

APRIL 2023

--- EVENTS---	--- TOP PRIORITIES---
	--- VARIOUS TO DO---
	--- PEOPLE TO CONNECT WITH---
	--- PLACES TO VISIT---
	--- THINGS FOR NEXT MONTH---

CHECKLIST-APRIL

ITEM:	DATE:	DONE:

NOTES:

Notes…

May 2023

Sun	Mon	Tue	Wed	Thu	Fri	Sat
	1	2	3	4	5	6
7	8	9	10	11	12	13
14	15	16	17	18	19	20
21	22	23	24	25	26	27
28	29	30	31			

MAY 2023

--- EVENTS---	--- TOP PRIORITIES---
	--- VARIOUS TO DO---
	--- PEOPLE TO CONNECT WITH---
	--- PLACES TO VISIT---
	--- THINGS FOR NEXT MONTH---

CHECKLIST-MAY

ITEM:	DATE:	DONE:

NOTES:

Notes…

I DRANK ALL THE WATER FROM MY BOWL BUT JUST NOW, IT IS FULL AGAIN

IT'S DOIN ME A FRIGHTEN

The hooman said we could go on a car ride tomorrow when he gets home. I'm so happy, I can't even snooze.

TAIL IS WAGGING SO FAST!

Photo

June 2023

Sun	Mon	Tue	Wed	Thu	Fri	Sat
				1	2	3
4	5	6	7	8	9	10
11	12	13	14	15	16	17
18	19	20	21	22	23	24
25	26	27	28	29	30	

JUNE 2023

--- EVENTS---

--- TOP PRIORITIES---

--- VARIOUS TO DO---

--- PEOPLE TO CONNECT WITH---

--- PLACES TO VISIT---

--- THINGS FOR NEXT MONTH---

CHECKLIST-JUNE

ITEM:	DATE:	DONE:

NOTES:

Notes…

MY THICKBOI
FREN THEODORE
FROM NEXT DOOR
STOLE THE SOCKS
I STOLE

HECKIN'
RUDE

Sweet Potato Fries Treats

Ingredients:
- 1 Sweet Potato
- 1 tbsp Coconut Oil (melted)
- Spices - Turmeric, Cinnamon

Instructions:

Preheat oven to 425 degrees F.

Wash and peel the sweet potato.

Cut the sweet potato into evenly sized long skinny (fry shaped) pieces.

Coat with oil and spices - Mix in a large bowl or Ziploc bag.

Place fries on baking sheet in one layer.

Bake for 15 minutes.

Flip over fries for even baking.

Bake for another 10-15 minutes.

Let cool before giving to your dog!

Dog Safe Spices
Basil. Cinnamon
Coriander, Dill
Ginger, Marjoram
Oregano, Parsley,
Rosemary, Sage
Tarragon, Thyme
Turmeric

July 2023

Sun	Mon	Tue	Wed	Thu	Fri	Sat
						1
2	3	4	5	6	7	8
9	10	11	12	13	14	15
16	17	18	19	20	21	22
23	24	25	26	27	28	29
30	31					

JULY 2023

--- EVENTS---

--- TOP PRIORITIES---

--- VARIOUS TO DO---

--- PEOPLE TO CONNECT WITH---

--- PLACES TO VISIT---

--- THINGS FOR NEXT MONTH---

CHECKLIST-JULY

ITEM:	DATE:	DONE:

NOTES:

Notes…

I COLLECTED ALL OF MY BALLS & SHOWED MY NEW FREN, LEON HOW TO HOLD THEM ALL IN HIS MOUTH

He's only little - He could only do one

August 2023

Sun	Mon	Tue	Wed	Thu	Fri	Sat
		1	2	3	4	5
6	7	8	9	10	11	12
13	14	15	16	17	18	19
20	21	22	23	24	25	26
27	28	29	30	31		

AUGUST 2023

--- TOP PRIORITIES---

--- VARIOUS TO DO---

--- PEOPLE TO CONNECT WITH---

--- PLACES TO VISIT---

--- THINGS FOR NEXT MONTH---

CHECKLIST-AUGUST

ITEM:	DATE:	DONE:

NOTES:

Notes…

THE HOOMAN HAS A NEW FREN OVER.

IF I AM IGNORED, I WILL NOTIFY THE FREN WITH A SERIES OF DISCRETE BORKS

EITHER PAT MY NOGGIN OR GIVE ME PEANUT BUTTER

BORK BOOF GRR BORK

September 2023

Sun	Mon	Tue	Wed	Thu	Fri	Sat
					1	2
3	4	5	6	7	8	9
10	11	12	13	14	15	16
17	18	19	20	21	22	23
24	25	26	27	28	29	30

SEPTEMBER 2023

--- EVENTS---	--- TOP PRIORITIES---
	--- VARIOUS TO DO---
	--- PEOPLE TO CONNECT WITH---
	--- PLACES TO VISIT---
	--- THINGS FOR NEXT MONTH---

CHECKLIST-SEPTEMBER

ITEM:	DATE:	DONE:

NOTES:

Notes…

October 2023

Sun	Mon	Tue	Wed	Thu	Fri	Sat
1	2	3	4	5	6	7
8	9	10	11	12	13	14
15	16	17	18	19	20	21
22	23	24	25	26	27	28
29	30	31				

OCTOBER 2023

--- EVENTS---

--- TOP PRIORITIES---

--- VARIOUS TO DO---

--- PEOPLE TO CONNECT WITH---

--- PLACES TO VISIT---

--- THINGS FOR NEXT MONTH---

CHECKLIST-OCTOBER

ITEM:	DATE:	DONE:

NOTES:

Notes…

MY TOP AGGRAVATIONS

BORIS, THE PESKY CAT

THE SPINNY MACHINE

LEASH TANGLES

CRUNCH WATER

INSIDE OUT EAR FLAPS

STICKS THAT BREAK

TAKE NOTE, HOOMAN

November 2023

Sun	Mon	Tue	Wed	Thu	Fri	Sat
			1	2	3	4
5	6	7	8	9	10	11
12	13	14	15	16	17	18
19	20	21	22	23	24	25
26	27	28	29	30		

NOVEMBER 2023

--- EVENTS---	--- TOP PRIORITIES---
	--- VARIOUS TO DO---
	--- PEOPLE TO CONNECT WITH---
	--- PLACES TO VISIT---
	--- THINGS FOR NEXT MONTH---

CHECKLIST-NOVEMBER

ITEM:	DATE:	DONE:

NOTES:

Notes...

Peppermint Holi-Dog Treats

Ingredients:

- 3 cups whole wheat flour
- 1 cup water
- 1 tsp molasses
- 2 Tbs peanut butter
- 2 Tbs olive oil
- 1 tsp peppermint extract

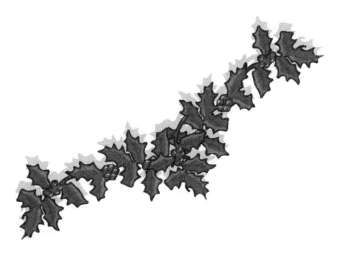

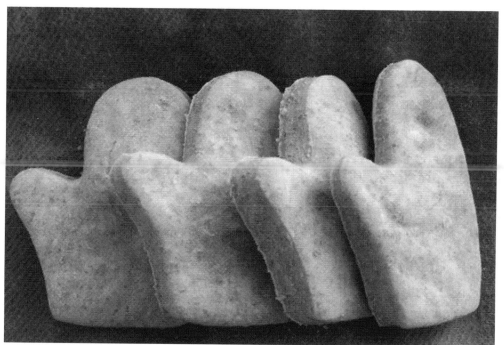

Instructions:

Preheat oven to 350 degrees.

In a large bowl, mix flour, molasses, peanut butter, water, olive oil and peppermint extract until smooth.

Kneed flour on a floured surface and roll out to ¼ inch thickness. Cut with festive cookie cutters and place on non-stick cookie sheets.

Bake for 30 minutes. Cool on wire rack. Store treats in a sealed container and refrigerate or freeze.

December 2023

Sun	Mon	Tue	Wed	Thu	Fri	Sat
					1	2
3	4	5	6	7	8	9
10	11	12	13	14	15	16
17	18	19	20	21	22	23
24	25	26	27	28	29	30
31						

DECEMBER 2023

--- EVENTS---	--- TOP PRIORITIES---
	--- VARIOUS TO DO---
	--- PEOPLE TO CONNECT WITH---
	--- PLACES TO VISIT---
	--- THINGS FOR NEXT MONTH---

CHECKLIST-DECEMBER

ITEM:	DATE:	DONE:

NOTES:

Notes…

SOMETIMES, MY HOOMAN WILL LIFT UP MY EAR FLAP AND SCRATCH MY NOGGIN

GYY

THIS IS COMPLETELY UNNECESSARY

2024

January

Su	Mo	Tu	We	Th	Fr	Sa
	1	2	3	4	5	6
7	8	9	10	11	12	13
14	15	16	17	18	19	20
21	22	23	24	25	26	27
28	29	30	31			

February

Su	Mo	Tu	We	Th	Fr	Sa
				1	2	3
4	5	6	7	8	9	10
11	12	13	14	15	16	17
18	19	20	21	22	23	24
25	26	27	28	29		

March

Su	Mo	Tu	We	Th	Fr	Sa
					1	2
3	4	5	6	7	8	9
10	11	12	13	14	15	16
17	18	19	20	21	22	23
24	25	26	27	28	29	30
31						

April

Su	Mo	Tu	We	Th	Fr	Sa
	1	2	3	4	5	6
7	8	9	10	11	12	13
14	15	16	17	18	19	20
21	22	23	24	25	26	27
28	29	30				

May

Su	Mo	Tu	We	Th	Fr	Sa
			1	2	3	4
5	6	7	8	9	10	11
12	13	14	15	16	17	18
19	20	21	22	23	24	25
26	27	28	29	30	31	

June

Su	Mo	Tu	We	Th	Fr	Sa
						1
2	3	4	5	6	7	8
9	10	11	12	13	14	15
16	17	18	19	20	21	22
23	24	25	26	27	28	29
30						

July

Su	Mo	Tu	We	Th	Fr	Sa
	1	2	3	4	5	6
7	8	9	10	11	12	13
14	15	16	17	18	19	20
21	22	23	24	25	26	27
28	29	30	31			

August

Su	Mo	Tu	We	Th	Fr	Sa
				1	2	3
4	5	6	7	8	9	10
11	12	13	14	15	16	17
18	19	20	21	22	23	24
25	26	27	28	29	30	31

September

Su	Mo	Tu	We	Th	Fr	Sa
1	2	3	4	5	6	7
8	9	10	11	12	13	14
15	16	17	18	19	20	21
22	23	24	25	26	27	28
29	30					

October

Su	Mo	Tu	We	Th	Fr	Sa
		1	2	3	4	5
6	7	8	9	10	11	12
13	14	15	16	17	18	19
20	21	22	23	24	25	26
27	28	29	30	31		

November

Su	Mo	Tu	We	Th	Fr	Sa
					1	2
3	4	5	6	7	8	9
10	11	12	13	14	15	16
17	18	19	20	21	22	23
24	25	26	27	28	29	30

December

Su	Mo	Tu	We	Th	Fr	Sa
1	2	3	4	5	6	7
8	9	10	11	12	13	14
15	16	17	18	19	20	21
22	23	24	25	26	27	28
29	30	31				

GOALS 2024

GOAL	MAKE IT HAPPEN

GOAL	MAKE IT HAPPEN

GOAL	MAKE IT HAPPEN

GOALS 2024

GOAL	MAKE IT HAPPEN

GOAL	MAKE IT HAPPEN

GOAL	MAKE IT HAPPEN

HOLIDAYS 2024

Monday, January 1	New Year's Day
Monday, January 15	Birthday of Martin Luther King, Jr.
Friday, Feb 2	Groundhog Day
Saturday, Feb 10	Chinese New Year
Wednesday, Feb 14	Valentine's Day
Monday, Feb 19	Washington's Birthday
Monday, March 11 (UK/CAN)	Commonwealth Day
Sunday, March 17	St. Patrick's Day
Sunday, March 10 (UK)	Mother's Day
Friday, March 29	Good Friday
Sunday, March 31	Easter Sunday
Monday, April 1	Easter Monday
Sunday, April 21	Queen's Birthday
Sunday, May 5	Cinco de Mayo
Wednesday, May 1	May Day
Monday, May 6 (UK)	Early May Bank Holiday
Sunday, May 12 (US/CAN)	Mother's Day
Monday, May 20 (CAN)	Victoria Day
Monday, May 27 (UK)	Spring Bank Holiday
Monday, May 27 (US)	Memorial Day
Sunday, June 16 (UK/US/CAN)	Father's Day
Monday, July 1	Canada Day
Thursday, July 4	Independence Day
Sunday, July 14	Bastille Day
Monday, September 2 (US/CAN)	Labor Day
Monday, Oct 14	Columbus Day Thanksgiving (CAN)
Thursday, Oct 31	Halloween
Monday, Nov 11 (US/UK)	Veteran's Day Remembrance Day
Tuesday, Nov 5 (UK)	Guy Fawkes Night
Thursday, Nov 28	Thanksgiving Day
Wednesday, Dec 25	Christmas Day
Thursday, Dec 26	Boxing Day
Tuesday, Dec 31	New Year's Eve

Hardwood floors are not ideal for doin' the zoomies. No traction anywhere. This situation needs to be remedied, hooman.

EAR FLAPS STUCK IN THE COUCH.!

Photo

January 2024

Sun	Mon	Tue	Wed	Thu	Fri	Sat
	1	2	3	4	5	6
7	8	9	10	11	12	13
14	15	16	17	18	19	20
21	22	23	24	25	26	27
28	29	30	31			

JANUARY 2024

--- EVENTS---

--- TOP PRIORITIES---

--- VARIOUS TO DO---

--- PEOPLE TO CONNECT WITH---

--- PLACES TO VISIT---

--- THINGS FOR NEXT MONTH---

CHECKLIST-JANUARY

ITEM:	DATE:	DONE:

NOTES:

Notes…

SOMETIMES, I MAKE A SMALL BOOF TO LET MY HOOMAN KNOW I NEED TO GO OUTSIDE.

THEN I JUST STAND IN THE DOORWAY & SNIFF THE AIR

HECKIN BAMBOOZLED

February 2024

Sun	Mon	Tue	Wed	Thu	Fri	Sat
				1	2	3
4	5	6	7	8	9	10
11	12	13	14	15	16	17
18	19	20	21	22	23	24
25	26	27	28	29		

FEBRUARY 2024

--- EVENTS---	--- TOP PRIORITIES---
	--- VARIOUS TO DO---
	--- PEOPLE TO CONNECT WITH---
	--- PLACES TO VISIT---
	--- THINGS FOR NEXT MONTH---

CHECKLIST-FEBRUARY

ITEM:	DATE:	DONE:

NOTES:

Notes…

March 2024

Sun	Mon	Tue	Wed	Thu	Fri	Sat
					1	2
3	4	5	6	7	8	9
10	11	12	13	14	15	16
17	18	19	20	21	22	23
24	25	26	27	28	29	30
31						

MARCH 2024

--- EVENTS---

--- TOP PRIORITIES---

--- VARIOUS TO DO---

--- PEOPLE TO CONNECT WITH---

--- PLACES TO VISIT---

--- THINGS FOR NEXT MONTH---

CHECKLIST-MARCH

ITEM:	DATE:	DONE:

NOTES:

Notes…

SOMETHING HAS WOKEN ME FROM MY AFTERNOON SNOOZLE

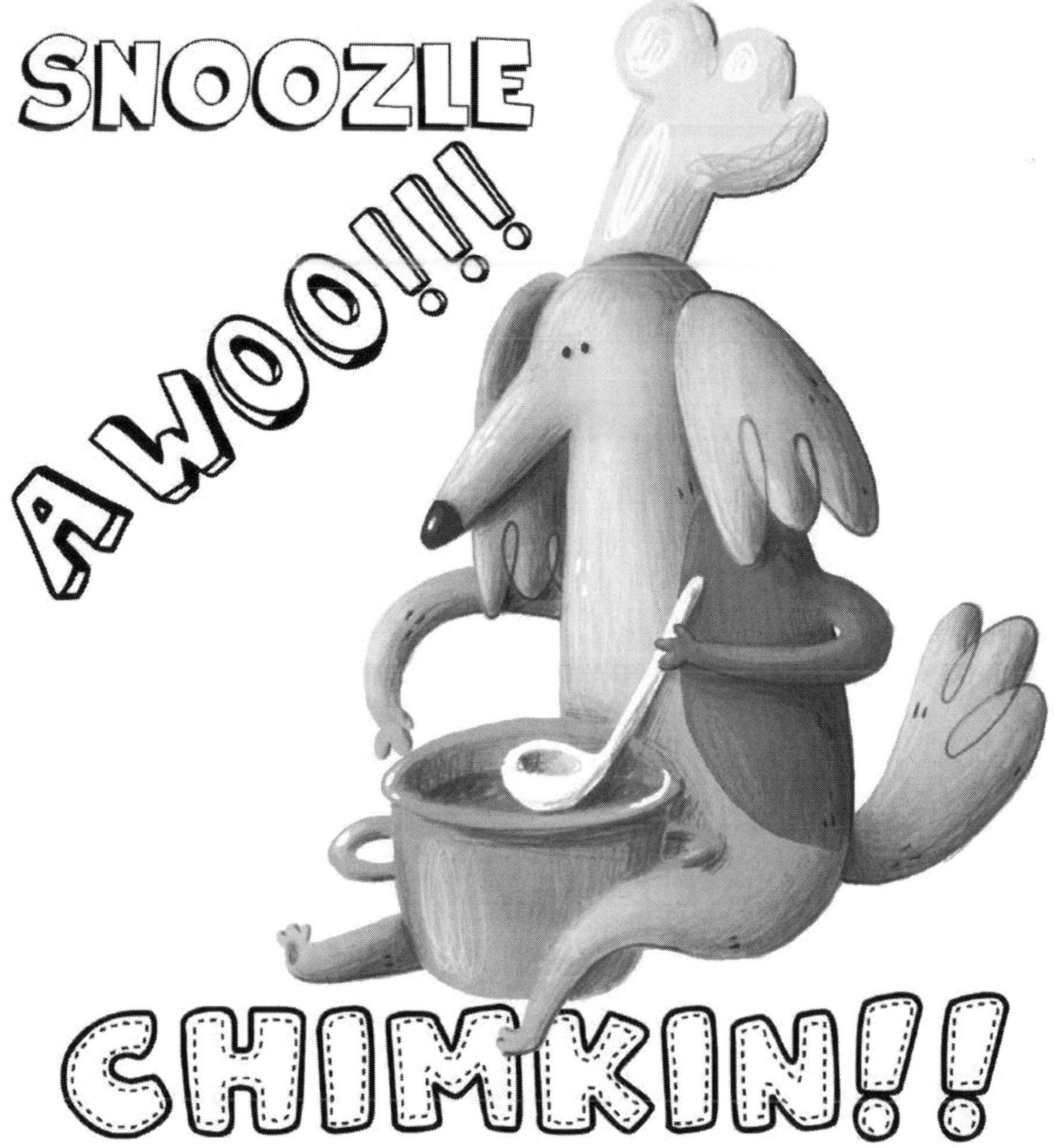

April 2024

Sun	Mon	Tue	Wed	Thu	Fri	Sat
	1	2	3	4	5	6
7	8	9	10	11	12	13
14	15	16	17	18	19	20
21	22	23	24	25	26	27
28	29	30				

APRIL 2024

--- EVENTS---

--- TOP PRIORITIES---

--- VARIOUS TO DO---

--- PEOPLE TO CONNECT WITH---

--- PLACES TO VISIT---

--- THINGS FOR NEXT MONTH---

CHECKLIST-APRIL

ITEM:	DATE:	DONE:

NOTES:

Notes…

LET ME TELL YOU ABOUT MY BEST STUFFED FREN, JEREMY

HE'S MY BESTEST PAL

HE'S GOT A LONG SNOOT FLOPPY EAR FLAPS

HE AGREES WITH EVERYTHING I SAY

May 2024

Sun	Mon	Tue	Wed	Thu	Fri	Sat
			1	2	3	4
5	6	7	8	9	10	11
12	13	14	15	16	17	18
19	20	21	22	23	24	25
26	27	28	29	30	31	

MAY 2024

--- EVENTS---	--- TOP PRIORITIES---
	--- VARIOUS TO DO---
	--- PEOPLE TO CONNECT WITH---
	--- PLACES TO VISIT---
	--- THINGS FOR NEXT MONTH---

CHECKLIST-MAY

ITEM:	DATE:	DONE:

NOTES:

Notes…

THE EVENING SNOOZLE IS FAST APPROACHING

DO NOT FORGET THE DOUBLE NOGGIN PAT INDICATING SWEET DREAMS

My most fancy tricks...
Snoozing, sit (a classic), the fetch,
trot/advanced walk, roll, zoom
(speedy), begging for chimkin.

SORTED BY DIFFICULTY!

Photo

Pumpkin Apple Dog Treats

Ingredients:

- 4 - 4.5 cups oatmeal, plus additional
- 1 medium apple
- 1 egg
- 1 CUP canned pumpkin

Instructions:

Preheat oven to 400 degrees F.

Grind the oatmeal down in a food processor or blender. Transfer to mixing bowl.

Core apple, being sure to remove all of the seeds. Grate apple, and add to bowl with oatmeal.

Add egg and canned pumpkin to bowl and mix well to combine. The mixture will be thick and slightly sticky.

On a surface dusted with oatmeal (ground or not, your choice) roll the dough out to approximately 1/2" thick. Use a doggy bone cookie cutter to cut dough into shapes, and transfer to a lined baking sheet.

Bake for approximately 12-15 minutes, or until golden and crispy. Allow to cool to room temperature, then store in an airtight container for up to a week.

June 2024

Sun	Mon	Tue	Wed	Thu	Fri	Sat
						1
2	3	4	5	6	7	8
9	10	11	12	13	14	15
16	17	18	19	20	21	22
23	24	25	26	27	28	29
30						

JUNE 2024

--- EVENTS---

--- TOP PRIORITIES---

--- VARIOUS TO DO---

--- PEOPLE TO CONNECT WITH---

--- PLACES TO VISIT---

--- THINGS FOR NEXT MONTH---

CHECKLIST-JUNE

ITEM:	DATE:	DONE:

NOTES:

Notes…

July 2024

Sun	Mon	Tue	Wed	Thu	Fri	Sat
	1	2	3	4	5	6
7	8	9	10	11	12	13
14	15	16	17	18	19	20
21	22	23	24	25	26	27
28	29	30	31			

JULY 2024

--- EVENTS---

--- TOP PRIORITIES---

--- VARIOUS TO DO---

--- PEOPLE TO CONNECT WITH---

--- PLACES TO VISIT---

--- THINGS FOR NEXT MONTH---

JULY 2024

CHECKLIST-JULY

ITEM:	DATE:	DONE:

NOTES:

Notes...

August 2024

Sun	Mon	Tue	Wed	Thu	Fri	Sat
				1	2	3
4	5	6	7	8	9	10
11	12	13	14	15	16	17
18	19	20	21	22	23	24
25	26	27	28	29	30	31

AUGUST 2024

--- EVENTS---

--- TOP PRIORITIES---

--- VARIOUS TO DO---

--- PEOPLE TO CONNECT WITH---

--- PLACES TO VISIT---

--- THINGS FOR NEXT MONTH---

CHECKLIST-AUGUST

ITEM:	DATE:	DONE:

NOTES:

Notes...

I HAVE NO PLANS
TODAY
JUST SNOOZLES
AND SNACKS

I CANCELLED MY PLANS
WITH MY FLOOFER
FREN, TIMBO
ABOUT HOW TO DO

MAXIMUM
ZOOMIES

ON HARD WOOD
FLOORS

September 2024

Sun	Mon	Tue	Wed	Thu	Fri	Sat
1	2	3	4	5	6	7
8	9	10	11	12	13	14
15	16	17	18	19	20	21
22	23	24	25	26	27	28
29	30					

SEPTEMBER 2024

--- EVENTS---

--- TOP PRIORITIES---

--- VARIOUS TO DO---

--- PEOPLE TO CONNECT WITH---

--- PLACES TO VISIT---

--- THINGS FOR NEXT MONTH---

CHECKLIST-SEPTEMBER

ITEM:	DATE:	DONE:

NOTES:

Notes…

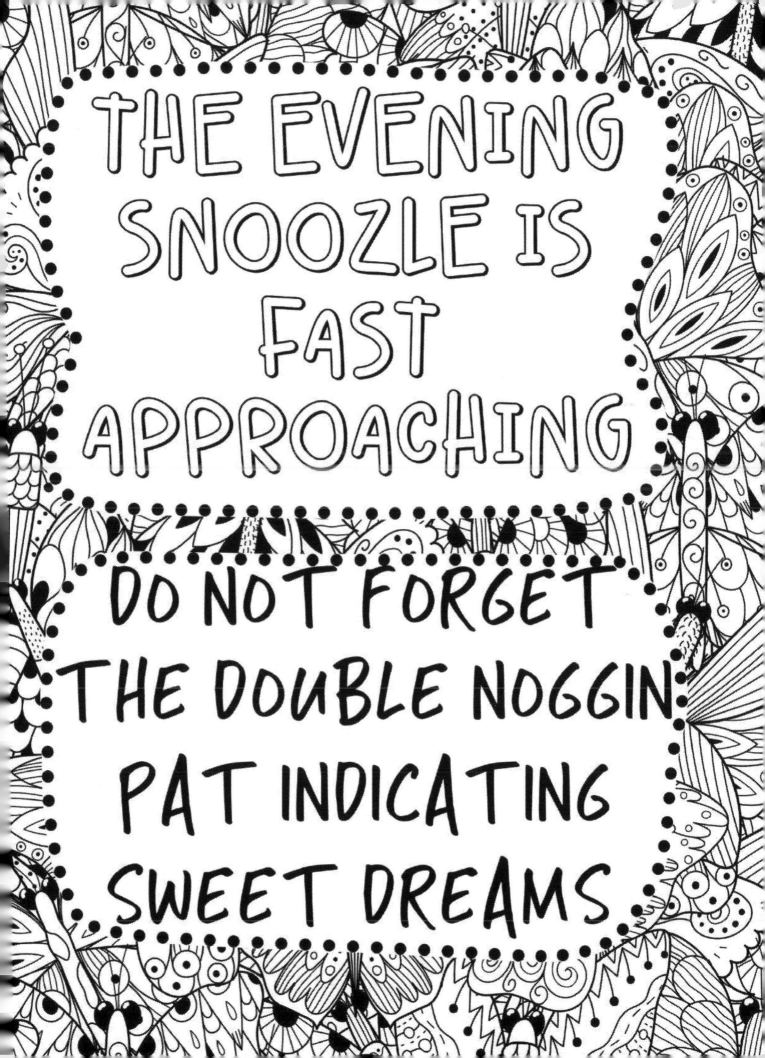

October 2024

Sun	Mon	Tue	Wed	Thu	Fri	Sat
		1	2	3	4	5
6	7	8	9	10	11	12
13	14	15	16	17	18	19
20	21	22	23	24	25	26
27	28	29	30	31		

OCTOBER 2024

--- EVENTS---

--- TOP PRIORITIES---

--- VARIOUS TO DO---

--- PEOPLE TO CONNECT WITH---

--- PLACES TO VISIT---

--- THINGS FOR NEXT MONTH---

CHECKLIST-OCTOBER

ITEM:	DATE:	DONE:

NOTES:

Notes…

November 2024

Sun	Mon	Tue	Wed	Thu	Fri	Sat
					1	2
3	4	5	6	7	8	9
10	11	12	13	14	15	16
17	18	19	20	21	22	23
24	25	26	27	28	29	30

NOVEMBER 2024

--- EVENTS---

--- TOP PRIORITIES---

--- VARIOUS TO DO---

--- PEOPLE TO CONNECT WITH---

--- PLACES TO VISIT---

--- THINGS FOR NEXT MONTH---

CHECKLIST-NOVEMBER

ITEM:	DATE:	DONE:

NOTES:

Notes…

Sometimes, I grrbork at the sky... in case anybody is listening.
You ever wake up in the middle of the night and think...why?

I NEED CHIMKIN!

Photo

Grain-Free Dog Treats

Ingredients:
- 2 cups coconut flour
- ½ teaspoon baking soda
- ½ teaspoon cinnamon
- 1 can 15 oz. pure pumpkin
- ½ cup peanut butter
- ½ cup coconut oil melted
- 4 eggs

Peanut Butter Drizzle:
- 1/3 cup peanut butter
- 1-2 tablespoons melted coconut oil

Instructions:

Preheat oven to 350 degrees F.

Add eggs to large bowl and beat. Add the remaining ingredients and stir together until a soft dough forms.

Place on parchment paper and carefully roll dough out with a rolling pin (you may need to put another piece of parchment paper on top so it doesn't stick to rolling pin).

Cut dough into shapes with cookie cutters and gently transfer to baking sheet lined with parchment paper.

Bake for 12 to 18 minutes, or until treats are hard. Remove from oven and cool for 5 minutes on baking sheet. Transfer to cooling rack.

For peanut butter drizzle, combine melted coconut oil and peanut butter and drizzle over treats.

Store in airtight container at room temperature or in the refrigerator up to one week. Store in the freezer for a month.

THE HOUSE TREE BROUGHT GIFTS WHICH IS DOIN' ME A BAMBOOZLE

I AM THE ONLY GIFT MY HOOMAN NEEDS

December 2024

Sun	Mon	Tue	Wed	Thu	Fri	Sat
1	2	3	4	5	6	7
8	9	10	11	12	13	14
15	16	17	18	19	20	21
22	23	24	25	26	27	28
29	30	31				

DECEMBER 2024

--- EVENTS---

--- TOP PRIORITIES---

--- VARIOUS TO DO---

--- PEOPLE TO CONNECT WITH---

--- PLACES TO VISIT---

--- THINGS FOR NEXT MONTH---

CHECKLIST-DECEMBER

ITEM:	DATE:	DONE:

NOTES:

Notes…

Printed in Great Britain
by Amazon